i

ISBN-13:
978-1456417277

ISBN-10:
1456417274

DEDICATION

To Billy and Peanut – two beautiful men
who embodied what it means to live and love
fully, completely, unconditionally and with
no questions asked.

To my parents, who may never understand,
but who are doing their very best.

To every child of God looking for a reason to keep
going – may this be one light among many to show
you the way.

To Lisa, Lucia, Gavi, Kaki and Bex.
For everything.

To Kendall.
For finding me. And for not letting go.

TABLE OF CONTENTS

And the young gay people in the Altoona, Pennsylvanias and the Richmond, Minnesotas who are coming out and hear Anita Bryant in television and her story. The only thing they have to look forward to is hope.

And you have to give them hope. Hope for a better world, hope for a better tomorrow, hope for a better place to come to if the pressures at home are too great. Hope that all will be all right.

Without hope, not only gays, but the blacks, the seniors, the handicapped, the us'es, the us'es will give up. And if you help elect to the central committee and other offices, more gay people, that gives a green light to all who feel disenfranchised, a green light to move forward. It means hope to a nation that has given up, because if a gay person makes it, the doors are open to everyone.

-- Harvey Milk. The "Hope Speech" March 10th, 1978

When someone asks me, "are gay rights civil rights?" my answer is always, "Of course, they are."

Civil rights are positive legal prerogatives: the right to equal treatment before the law. These are the rights shared by everyone. There is no one in the United States who does not, or should not, enjoy or share in enjoying these rights.

Gay and lesbian rights are not special rights in any way. It isn't "special" to be free from discrimination. It is an ordinary, universal entitlement of citizenship.

-- National NAACP Chairman Julian Bond
in a speech at the Human Rights Campaign's
Los Angeles Dinner on Saturday, March 14 2009

I know African Americans, they get upset. They're like, 'black and gay, that's totally different things. We had it hard.' And I'm like, 'yeah, I get it. I'm black. I know. I get it. You know.

But there's things that gay people have to go through that black people didn't have to go through. I never had to come out black. Never had to sit my family down and tell them about my blackness. Have a little talk with my employer, let him know about my 'black lifestyle.' Mom, Dad, I gotta tell you something. Hope you still love me. I'm black. You know, and my mother: 'Not black, Lord! Anything but black, Jesus! Anything but black! What did I do, what did I do? It was "Soul Train," wasn't it? I shouldn't have let you watch "Soul Train."' No, ma, that's just me--I mean, I just feel like I was born black. 'No, you weren't born black. The bible says Adam and Eve; it doesn't say Adam and Mary J. Blige.'

*-- Wanda Sykes on 'The Ellen DeGeneres Show" in 2008
after the passage of Proposition 8, which took
away the right to gay marriage in California*

ACKNOWLEDGEMENTS

While the African-American experience is often lost in the conversation about what it means to be lesbian, gay, bisexual or transgender (LGBT) in today's culture, the gifted artists, entertainers, thinkers and community leaders profiled here remind us all that our community exists in many forms.

This book is an exploration of what it means to be a part of LGBT culture, and a part of African-American culture, at the same time.

Originally inspired by Lorraine Hansberry's book To Be Young, Gifted and Black, *as well as* I Dream A World, *the groundbreaking book of African-American portraiture,* Black, Gifted and Gay *highlights portraits of twenty African-American icons who have had the courage to publicly claim their place in the LGBT community.*

The courage, commitment and accomplishments of these ground-breaking men and women serve as an inspiration to us all.

TO BE BLACK, GIFTED AND GAY

BY LEYLA FARAH

It hasn't always been this way.

There was a time when black people, and people who identified as lesbian, gay, bisexual and transgender ("LGBT," or just "gay") – and people who happened to be both – shared the same space in the minds of their straight, white counterparts. There was a time when we sought refuge with one another – safe from the shared loathing we each faced elsewhere.

We shared nightclubs, art, literature and politics. We challenged the status quo and broke new ground – delighting audiences, creating beauty, and defining the discourse of the day. We were each, in our own way, unfettered. We had the freedom to explore expression in all forms - and we were each compelled to express both the painful nature and the raw joy of our exiled existence.   We shared the natural alliance of the unwanted and the maligned. We each lacked access to the levers of social power. We each faced the daily likelihood of a sudden and violent death. We shared what we had and we shared what we feared. We found solace in one another.

In the 1920's and 1930's - the era of the Harlem Renaissance – black and gay thinkers, artists and writers defined the texture of American society. By the 1960's – the era of the civil rights movement – those social textures had shifted dramatically. The subtle, social changes of the intervening years redefined the landscape of the original alliance. Black people were making real strides – however painfully – towards accessing the social prerogatives so long denied them. Hard fought battles for social justice were waged and – for the most part – won. Gradual, often almost imperceptible, changes began to add up to larger victories. Progress became palpable. The heavy burdens of life outside of the mainstream of American culture slowly – very slowly – began to lift.

The fact that the progress being made by the civil rights movement was visibly led by the black church, elevated black religious leaders to the status of social leaders. The two roles became conceptually synonymous, and culturally equivalent. Voices from the church supplanted voices from the fields of politics, art, literature and academia almost entirely.

The memory that black and gay cultures had once overlapped by virtue of their shared rejection from the heterosexual white mainstream began to fade. Church rhetoric shaped the language of the civil rights movement. In the context of divine will, controversial and alternative thought had little value. The nightclubs and speakeasies that had served as gathering places for gay people and black people – and those that happened to be both – had no place in the pious backdrop so painstakingly painted by those at the forefront of the movement.

More importantly, it became clear that continued association with the freewheeling underground of the day only undermined the goals the fathers of the civil rights movement were fighting so hard to achieve.

It was a clear choice. The gays had to go. Whether real or imagined, the possibility that the first glimmer of social and cultural progress for black people might be threatened by a continued association with a group still maligned by the rest of the country was a risk no one felt compelled to take. The divide grew wider. Those who carried memories of a time when things had been different died without leaving a record of that alliance behind.

Twenty years later, when AIDS ravaged gay people in the 1980s, the alliance was lost completely. Black clergy, and by extension the default leadership of black cultural thought, spoke out early and often against the moral depravity of gay people and its connection to the prevalence of the disease. The bible became a weapon in the hands of both black clergy and white – wielded openly and with a ferocity and conviction not seen since it was used to justify the enslavement of black people themselves.

Those who happened to be both black and gay now found themselves confronted by a unified message of condemnation emanating from the leadership of their own community.

While there had once been social constructs in the black community that allowed for same sex relationships – although not commonly labeled as such – any appearance of homosexuality quickly became dangerous. Gender roles for black men and women, already impacted by the legacy of slavery, began to further exaggerate elements of heterosexuality. Black men were celebrated for their sexual conquest of women, black women for their sexual availability to men. The "pimp" and "ho" archetypes became embedded into the social fabric of the black community.

After the abundant contributions made by those who were both black and gay during the Harlem Renaissance, contributions by those who actively claimed both the black and gay communities disappear from the record almost entirely. As those in the mainstream gay movement were exhorting one another to come out of the closet and participate in public events and parades, black faces were rarely seen in the crowd. Activists and organizers – with a few key exceptions – were almost always white.

The art and literature of the day shows little evidence of their existence as part of the civil rights movement in either the black or gay communities. There are long stretches of American history where black, gay people are essentially absent from the struggles, stories and accomplishments that define either the gay or black communities. Those heroes we do celebrate – Audre Lorde, James Baldwin, Bayard Rustin, and other giants of their era – are long dead.

This book is an effort – however small – to address that absence. Collecting the profiles of these twenty living icons, who are both black and openly gay, is one way to ensure that the contributions of black, gay people are not lost to future history books. It is one way to reclaim the intersection between two communities that once found strength with one another. It is one way to undo the decades of damage done by those who felt they had few other choices.

It is just one way, but with so much work to be done, at least it is one less thing to do.

LEE
DANIELS

50-year-old, openly-gay producer/director Lee Daniels was the first African American sole producer of an Academy Award-winning film for Monster's Ball (starring Halle Berry, Billy Bob Thornton and Heath Ledger).

The 2001 film about race, politics, feminism, and the legal system won a Screen Actors Guild Award (SAG) for Outstanding Performance by a Female Actor in a Leading Role (Halle Berry), two National Board of Review awards and a Black Reel Award. Monster's Ball was the first production from Lee Daniels Entertainment – a company started by Daniels. Prior to his work on Monster's Ball, Daniels worked as a casting director on the films Under the Cherry Moon and Purple Rain.

Following the success of Monster's Ball, Daniels produced the Kevin Bacon and Kyra Sedgwick film The Woodsman in 2004. He would make his directorial debut with the film Shadowboxer in 2006. Shadowboxer starred Helen

Mirren, Cuba Gooding, Jr., Mon'Nique, Joseph Gorden-Levitt, and Macy Gray (among others). 2008 would bring the film production of Tennessee starring Adam Rothenberg, Ethan Peck, Mariah Carey, and Lance Reddick.

Daniels teamed up again in 2009 with Mo'Nique and Mariah Carey for the two-time Academy Award-winning film Precious. The movie was based on the novel "Push" by Sapphire and depicted a tumultuous mother-daughter relationship on the brink of multiple emotional disasters. Daniels would be honored at the GLAAD Media Awards in 2010 for his work on the film and for being a celebrated gay black director in film.

Politically-speaking, Daniels produced public service announcements to urge young people of color to vote in 2004. The ads would feature LL Cool J and Alicia Keys.

Daniels has two adopted children and currently resides in New York City. His next feature film is based on the lives of Martin Luther King, Jr. and Lyndon Baines Johnson. It is slated to release in 2011 and is called Selma.

[1] *Photo by David Christopher Lee*

ANGELA DAVIS

Feminist political activist Angela Davis was born to a service station owner father and elementary school teacher mother on January 26, 1944. They lived in Birmingham, Alabama in the racially divided neighborhood known as "Dynamite Hill." Davis attended an all-black elementary school, middle school and high school before being accepted into an integrated Northern school in her junior year. She would have to relocate to New York City's Greenwich Village to attend. It was at Elisabeth Irwin High School that Davis would become interested in studying socialism.

Davis was one of only three black students at the Brandeis University in Waltham, Massachusetts. Around this time, Davis would cross paths with philosopher Herbert Marcuse during a rally regarding the Cuban Missile Crisis. She would travel next to France, Switzerland

and Finland before returning to Brandeis for her sophomore year. She would return to France to attend Hamilton College in her junior year and then partake in the study of philosophy in her senior year back at Brandeis. In 1965, David graduated magna cum laude as a member of Phi Beta Kappa . She would travel to Germany, live with a German family, study their culture and history, and then return to the United States, this time to San Diego, California, where she would eventually earn her master's degree and then her doctorate in philosophy from Humboldt University in California.

On August 7, 1970, Superior Court Judge Harold Haley, along with additional hostages, was abducted from his California courtroom and, ultimately, murdered. Davis was charged as an accomplice to conspiracy, kidnapping and homicide. On August 18, 1970, Davis became the third woman and the 309th person to appear on the FBI's Ten Most Wanted Fugitives List. She would flee the state and seek refuge in New York City until her capture. In 1972, she would be tried and found not guilty. Two songs were written in the same year by activist singer/songwriters after this incident. One was called "Angela" (written by John Lennon and Yoko Ono) and the other was called "Sweet Black Angel" by the Rolling Stones' Mick Jagger. Davis left for Cuba after the ordeal.

Davis' activism did not end there. In 1980 and 1984, she would run for Vice President on the Communist Party ticket. She would also win the Lenin Peace Prize from East Germany for her civil rights activism. She would help to create the grassroots organization Critical Resistance – dedicated to building a movement to abolish the prison system. She would also form the African American Agenda 2000 in support of black feminists.

An out-lesbian since 1997, Davis currently resides in New York City and is a Distinguished Visiting Professor in the Women's and Gender Studies Department at Syracuse University.

[2] *Photo by Nick Wiebe*

FELICIA "SNOOP" PEARSON

Openly-gay 30-year-old Baltimore, Maryland actress Felicia "Snoop" Pearson is a true example of what can happen when you work hard to make your life better – regardless of life circumstances thrust upon you at birth. Literally. Pearson was born a mere three pounds and was not expected to live. Both of her parents were incarcerated drug addicts. She would live with foster parents in East Baltimore and follow in her parents footsteps by skipping school to become a drug dealer herself.

At age 14, Pearson was convicted of second-degree murder. She was immediately sentenced to two eight year terms, to be served consecutively. She would serve five years of the sentence in the Maryland Correctional Institution for Women in Jessup, Maryland. While incarcerated, Pearson would successfully complete the GED program to obtain her high school diploma. Felicia fought the system every step of the way. It was the murder of her father figure, drug dealer Arnold Loney while she was in Jessup that changed things. She called him Uncle, he was the man who nicknamed Pearson "Snoop" after the Peanuts character. His death would change Pearson's life forever.

HBO's The Wire Actor Michael K. Williams spotted Pearson at a club one evening and asked her to audition for the show. He thought that she would be the perfect addition because of her over-sized swagger and attitude. Of the encounter, Williams said, "I got intoxicated with her. I saw her strength and her vulnerability. You look in her eyes and you see things... I said, 'This woman deserves a shot at something more than what the Baltimore streets have to offer.' I felt compelled to give her an option, just in case she wanted to try something else." That night would become the beginning of Pearson's acting career. Stephen King wrote in Entertainment Weekly, that the TV Snoop is "perhaps the most terrifying female villain to ever appear in a television series."

Felicia co-wrote the best selling book GRACE AFTER MIDNIGHT, a memoir, and looks forward to completing her second book, which is the first in a series about a gay woman holding her own in a man's world.

[3] *Photo courtesy Felicia "Snoop" Pearson*

ANDRÉ LEON TALLEY

American author and fashion icon André Leon Talley is perhaps best known for his role as an editor for Vogue magazine. He has mentored some of the most popular celebrities in the entertainment industry, including: Tracy Reese, Rachel Roy, Jennifer Hudson, Mariah Carey, Kimora Lee Simmons, and Venus Williams. His work as a judge on Tyra Banks' America's Next Top Model further cemented his prominent position in the fashion world.

Born in Durham, North Carolina on October 16, 1949, Talley was left to be raised by his grandmother. Talley attended North Carolina Central University and later received his master's degree in French from Brown University in Providence, Rhode Island. His first reported job was as an assistant to New York City artist and fashion icon Andy Warhol for $50.00 per week.

In 2003, Talley released his autobiography titled *A.L.T.: A Memoir*. Writing about his upbringing in Durham, Tally shared, "We always had clothes to wear and food on the table, but we lived on limited means. Our roof leaked buckets of water when the snow melted, and if the pipes froze, my grandmother heated water on the wood-burning stove so I could take a 'bird bath' before school." He also recalled how segregation and attacks on the black population hit close to home. He said that "for a long time my grandmother would not allow white people to come into our house. That was her rule. The only white man who ever came into the house was the coroner."

Talley has received awards throughout his career as an editor, journalist and fashion designer. Among them: Eugenia Sheppard Award and the Council of Fashion Designers of America, 2003, for fashion journalism.

When President Barack Obama was introduced to the world as the new Commander-in-Chief at the Inaugural Ball in 2008, his wife – First Lady Michelle Obama – was wearing a dress designed by relatively-new fashion designer Jason Wu. Talley was the conduit between the two forces and had made the first introduction.

[4] *Photo by David Shankbone*

MAURICE JAMAL

Maurice Jamal is recognized in the entertainment industry as being one of the few contemporary African American filmmakers to consistently profile the lives of the black community in film.

He wrote, directed and starred in the independent gay and lesbian romantic comedy *The Ski Trip* in 2005. *The Ski Trip* also starred John Rankin, Haaz Sleiman and Emanuel Xavier. The film put Jamal on the map for its wide range of appeal within the lesbian, gay, transgender, and bisexual (LGBT) community. It featured gay and lesbian characters of color in a comedy that was laugh out loud funny, but balanced with humanity. The film premier helped launch the LOGO Network in 2005, and was their sole programming featuring people of color until *Noah's Arc* debuted later that year.

In 2007, Jamal released his second film *Dirty Laundry* chronicling the story of a larger-than-life gay male character returning home to the south after living in the big city. Rockmond Dunbar, Loretta Devine, Jenifer Lewis, Sommore and Jamal himself topped off the cast of this hysterical family dramedy. The film made history as the first Black gay-themed family film to receive a theatrical release. 2009 brought his acclaimed digital series *Friends and Lovers*.

Jamal was raised in Berkeley, CA and had an understandably non-traditional educational experience in this bastion of progressive values. Admittedly an awkward teen, Jamal underwent a life-changing experience when Aaliyah's plane crashed in 2001. Of the event, Jamal shared, "I was friends with, and admired, a fellow artist who was on Aaliyah's plane. After his sudden death it caused me to reevaluate my life and decide to really walk my path."

"My friend [Anthony] had always talked about moving to LA and getting in the business. I realized that life is short and firmly believe that God wants us to be happy and the universe wants us to utilize our gifts and talents. So I got off the pot – I bought a one-way ticket to New York City and pursued acting and directing full time. Even more, I did it without a Plan B because for me having a Plan B means you are considering the possibility of failing."

Jamal has been profiled in Black Enterprise Magazine, Essence, JET, Variety, OUT magazine and The Advocate and is listed in BET's "Who's Who in Black LGBT America." Jamal supports many charitable causes and speaks nationally on the issues of HIV/AIDS, youth empowerment and LGBT community development. He sits on the Board of Directors of Frameline, the world's largest LGBT Film Festival; The Blackhouse Foundation, which supports the development of Black Independent Cinema; and

National Black Coming Out Day. Currently he is the Founder and President of GLO TV Network – the world's first Urban LGBT network.

"I'm so excited to be the President of GLO TV. I've had much success in this industry and I am glad that I have done so as an openly gay person of color. I've sold films to LOGO, worked at BET and Comedy Central, and I've had successful films on the big screen. But this is the most important thing I have ever done in my career. Every day I get messages from LGBT people all across this country… every race, young and old, who are living life and reaching for their dreams. Some have been inspired by a movie they've seen, or a book they've read. Some are dealing with the challenges of living an authentic life. But what we all have in common is our need to be seen and heard for who we truly are. GLO TV is more than just a network. GLO TV is US. It's OUR lives, OUR stories, OUR chance. I'm proud to take this journey with each and every one of you. It's time to let our light shine. It's time to get our "GLO on."

Up next is the hip-hop crime drama series SOLDIER, with a homoerotic twist and THE BIG MO SHOW, a political and pop culture talk show being hosted by Jamal.

[5] *Photo courtesy Maurice Jamal.*

EMIL WILBEKIN

Named one of OUT magazine's 100 Most Influential Gay People in 2002, Emil Wilbekin is perhaps best known for his 10-year tenure at Quincy Jones' Vibe magazine where he served as Editor-in-Chief and won a National Magazine Award. His flair for fashion, style, music, and pop culture propelled Wilbekin into the limelight and into the hearts of lesbian, gay, bisexual, and transgender people the world over.

Born in Cincinnati, Ohio in 1968, Wilbekin enrolled in college at Virginia's Hampton University before switching to New York's Columbia University's Graduate School of Journalism. In 2004, Wilbekin would be inducted into the Mass Media Arts Hall of Fame at Hampton University.

Wilbekin's journey on the pathway towards journalism excellence began with writing and editing stories in celebrated news and entertainment magazines, such as: People Magazine, Chicago Tribune, Associated Press, and Metropolitan Home. In 1992, he would join the Vibe team and seven years later, in 1999, he would become Vibe's Editor-in-Chief. Wilbekin would contribute to Vibe until 2004. While working with Vibe, Wilbekin garnered the 2002 National Magazine Award for General Excellence and helped build readership circulation to an estimated 825,000. Wilbekin also became Editorial Director/Vice President of Brand Development for Vibe Ventures where he served as an executive producer for the 1st Annual "Vibe Awards."

In 2005, Wilbekin transitioned over to Marc Ecko Enterprises to become the company's Vice President of Brand Development. He also became the Style Guru at Complex in that same year. Later, in 2008, he would become Editor-in-Chief of GIANT Magazine – an urban entertainment and lifestyle bi-monthly magazine promoting the best of music, film and fashion. He would move on to become Managing Editor of Essence.com in 2009.

Also focused on humanitarian work, Wilbekin serves on the board of directors for the American Society of Magazine Editors (ASME), the Design Industries Fighting AIDS (DIFFA), the Brotherhood SisterSol, 24 Hours for Life, and is a member of the Black AIDS institute. Among his numerous prestigious awards are: Pratt Institute's Creative Spirit Award, the Howard University Entertainment, Sports, and Law Club Media Award, The Anti Violence Project's Courage Award, and The Hetrick Martin Institute's Emory Award.

6 Photo courtesy Emil Wilbekin

PARIS BARCLAY

Multiple Emmy Award-winning director and producer Paris Barclay has worked on some of the world's finest television shows, including: NYPD Blue, ER, The West Wing, CSI, Lost, The Shield, House M.D., Law & Order, Monk, Numb3rs, City of Angels, Cold Case, The Mentalist, Weeds, Sons of Anarchy, NCIS: Los Angeles, The Good Wife, In Treatment, and Glee.

Barclay's immaculate work in the entertainment medium was recognized in the form of a Directors Guild of America (DGA) award for NYPD Blue as well as 10 DGA nominations. He was noted for being the first director in the history of the DGA to be nominated for a comedy series and drama series in the same year, two years in a row (2008 & 2009). Barclay also won the National Association for the Advancement of Colored People (NAACP) Image award for Best Drama Series as co-creator, writer, and director of City of Angels and another for directing Cold Case. His MTV film Pedro was nominated for a GLAAD Media Award as well as a Humanitas Prize.

An openly gay man, Barclay was born on June 30, 1956 in Chicago, Illinois. He attended the private college preparatory institution La Lumiere School on a scholarship and was one of the very first African Americans to do so. After graduating from Lumiere, Barclay would enroll in and graduate from Harvard University. His roommate was Memoirs of a Geisha novelist Arthur Golden.

Barclay currently serves as First Vice President of the DGA. He is the first African American officer in the history of the Guild.

[7] *Photo by Richard Berg*

E. DENISE SIMMONS

Cambridge, Massachusetts former mayor E. Denise Simmons was the first lesbian, African-American mayor in United States history. Adding to the landmark appointment was the fact that Simmons won the seat unanimously. Her term lasted from 2008-2009.

Simmons made the following statement following her election. "Just like being a Cantabrigian, a grandmother, a Justice of the Peace, a small business owner, and Mayor, being gay is part of who I am. I live in a city where my friends, family and colleagues just know me as Denise, not as the first African American lesbian mayor. One of the main reasons that public service has drawn me is that I believe in fairness and equality for all people, whether they are gay or straight, African American or of another background, women or men. Equity and access to services and opportunities is what raises all of us to a higher quality of life. I started the GLBT Commission in Cambridge for that reason, to engage the broader community in policy issues that would make Cambridge a better place to live and work for gay individuals and families. I'm proud of the progress the Commission has made. All of my work centers around civic engagement

– I truly believe that is how the strongest communities are built, on the vision, involvement and actions of their citizens. Although being a lesbian is not something that defines my work, I realize that this is a great step for the GLBT community and I am truly honored to have this opportunity to be a leader."

Simmons holds a Bachelor of Science degree in Sociology from the University of Massachusetts at Boston and a Master's degree in Psychotherapy from Antioch College. Her work in the Cambridge school system is notable and revered. After serving 12 years as the Executive Director of the Civic Unity Committee (a city-funded citizen rights organization), she earned a spot on the Cambridge School Committee in 1992. Her powerful work of expanding diversity throughout the school system helped propel her further into the community-driven goal of inclusion.

After winning a seat on the city council in 2001, Simmons utilized her successes to further the civil rights movement on behalf of the African American and lesbian, gay, bisexual, and transgender (LGBT) communities. In 2004, three years into her service, Cambridge City Hall became the first municipality to recognize and issue marriage licenses to same-sex couples.

[8] *Photo by Yoon S. Byun*

LZ GRANDERSON

Perhaps one of the the most visible sports journalists in the nation, LZ Granderson is African-American, openly-gay, Christian, and one of ESPN's most popular columnists. The one time Detroit gang member is now a sought-after commentator on pivotal topics such as race, gender and politics, in addition to sports.

Prior to joining ESPN first as a magazine editor and later as a writer, Mr. Granderson was a sports columnist for the Atlanta Journal-Constitution, and was the reporter to whom professional basketball player Sheryl Swoopes came out of the closet in 2005. He later joined ESPN360's talk show Game Night.

Now a force to be reckoned with at ESPN.com's Page 2 and ESPN the Magazine, Granderson sparked controversy in his July 16, 2009 CNN column titled "Gay is Not the New Black."

In the piece, Granderson wrote:
"In their minds, Obama is not moving fast enough on behalf of the GLBT community. The outcry is not

completely without merit — the Justice Department's unnerving brief on the Defense of Marriage Act immediately comes to mind. I was upset by some of the statements, but not surprised. (After the Tuskegee Syphilis Study, President Ronald Reagan's initial handling of AIDS and, more recently, Katrina, there is little that surprises me when it comes to the government and the treatment of its people). Still, rarely has criticism regarding Obama and the GLBT community come from the kind of person you would find standing in line at a spot like The Prop House, and there's a reason for that. Despite the catchiness of the slogan, gay is not the new black. Black is still black. And if any group should know this, it's the gay community."

The editorial journalist and activist was a Fellow at the Columbia University Hechinger Institute, is a member of the National Association of Black Journalists, and has served on the board for the National Lesbian and Gay Journalists Association. Granderson won awards for the 2008 Excellence in Journalism awards given by the National Lesbian and Gay Journalists Association and from The Gay & Lesbian Alliance Against Defamation (GLAAD) in 2009 for his contributions to online journalism.

[9] *Photo courtesy ESPN*

MESHELL NDEGEOCELLO

Credited in the media for having started the "neo-soul" movement, 42-year-old singer-songwriter Meshell Ndegeocello is a proud bisexual African American woman with ten Grammy Award nominations stowed in her satchel.

Born in Germany and raised in Washington, D.C., Ndegeocello started her music career by recording a self-made demo in her bedroom before taking off to New York City hoping to strike gold as a bassist. She was soon signed to Madonna's Maverick Records and she would release eight studio albums between the years of 1993 and 2009.

Tantalizing sounds, strikingly-authentic structures, and gnawingly raw lyrics lined the albums from the inside out and Ndegeocello's sound and passion caught immediate fire within the entertainment industry. The musician's ambiguous demeanor and representation of self further fueled media speculation into not only her music, but sexuality and social practices that were fairly taboo at the time of her arrival on the scene.

With her shaved head and sultry vocals Ndegeocello was the antithesis of R&B's more traditionally manicured divas, and her open bisexuality challenged virtually everyone. In an interview with the Los Angeles Times, she said, "I'm the ultimate misfit... I'm black. I'm a woman. I'm a bisexual."

In addition to her own studio recordings, Ndegeocello has contributed her vocal abilities and bass talent to artistic ventures by the Indigo Girls, The Rolling Stones, Alanis Morissette, Zap Mama, and Basement Jaxx. Perhaps one of her most popular hits came from a working relationship with John Cougar Mellencamp. The pair joined to release a cover of Van Morrison's "Wild Night" and it topped the Billboard charts at the #3 position in the summer of 1994.

Meshell has released 8 albums since 1993, including her most recent: Devil's Halo (Oct. 2009). She was one of the first artists signed to Madonna's Maverick Records, which released her first 5 albums.

Meshell has played on albums by The Rolling Stones, John Mellencamp, Madonna, Santana, The Blind Boys of Alabama, Guru's Jazzmatazz, Chaka Khan, Indigo Girls,

Ledisi, Alanis Morissette, Joan Osborne, Basement Jaxx, Soulive, Gilles Peterson, Joshua Redman Elastic Band and Karl Denson's Tiny Universe among many others. Her music has been featured on film soundtracks including Batman & Robin, Love Jones, Money Talks, Down in the Delta, How Stella Got Her Groove Back, The Hurricane, Love & Basketball, Standing in the Shadows of Motown, Talk to Me and Soul Men among others.

Although she has changed the spelling of her name over the past 20 years in the music business, "Ndegeocello" is the correct way to spell it currently. The name literally means "free like a bird." Ndegeocello's birth name is on record as "Michelle Lynn Johnson."

A bass player above all else, Meshell brings her signature warm, fat, and melodic groove to everything she does. Canonized, marginalized or just scrutinized, she has given up trying to explain herself. After 20+ years in an industry that has called her everything from avant garde to a dying breed, what unquestionably remains is the fearsome bassist, prolific songwriter and the creativity and curiosity of an authentic musical force. With that, she has earned critical acclaim, the unfailing respect of fellow players, songwriters and composers, and the dedication of her diverse, unclassifiable fans.

[10] *Photo by Mark Seliger.*

PATRIK·IAN POLK

Punks director, writer and producer Patrik-Ian Polk paved the way for gay black men and women with his successful grassroots efforts in the film and television mediums. Punks premiered in 2000 at the Sundance Film Festival and garnered multiple awards during its run on the Independent Film circuit. It was then released to theatres around the world in 2001.

The film starred Rockmond Dunbar, Renoly Santiago, Jazzmun, and Devon Odessa, and was produced with the help of "Babyface" [Kenneth Edmonds]. After the film's successful run, Polk decided to focus on television and create a groundbreaking series that would alter the structure of gay relationships in the media.

Working with the Human Rights Campaign (HRC) and the Black AIDS Institute, Noah's Arc focused on the black lesbian, gay, bisexual and transgender (LGBT) communities and the struggles faced within the walls of society and relationships. The poignant same-sex subject matter in every episode would play out with a total of two seasons from 2005 through 2006 on MTV's Logo network. Noah's Arc instantly became one of the most popular shows on Logo's television line-up in 2005. The show ultimately faced cancellation, but Polk released a follow-up film to please the fans and continue the storylines he had started and intended to share. Noah's Arc: Jumping the Broom would premiere in 2008.

Regarding his partnership with the Black AIDS Institute, Polk has said, "AIDS is like a dirty little secret in the Black community. I think people really appreciate the show [Noah's Arc]. The network understands the need to address this issue. The statistics are staggering in both the gay and straight Black communities. The problem can't be denied." He continued, "Any issues important to Black gay men are important to me. AIDS is the most important social and health issue today. I'll do anything I can as an artist to have a positive impact on a social level. My strength is my art."

The 37-year-old openly-gay Mississippi-born activist made the necessary rounds before fame came knocking at his door. Attending Brandeis University in Massachusetts before graduating from film school at the University of Southern California School of Cinema-Television, Polk first signed on to become a production assistant on the set of SeaQuest, DSV [Amblin Entertainment]. In the years following, Polk would move on to become a development executive at MTV Films and then, later, vice president of production and development at Edmonds Entertainment/e2 Filmworks. While there, he would work on the films Soul Food (starring Vanessa Williams, Vivica A. Fox and Nia Long), Hav Plenty (starring Chenoa Maxwell, Robinne Lee and Hill Harper) and Light It Up (starring Usher Raymond, Rosario Dawson, Forest Whitaker, and Vanessa L. Williams).

[11] *Photo originally published on BET.com*

KEVIN AVIANCE

28-year-old New York City underground club performer, Kevin Aviance (née – Eric Snead), was the first-ever drag queen to design and release a line of women's shoes. The gender-bending personality inherent in Aviance came to light when the young performer was in seventh grade donning female clothing for musical numbers he would perform at his junior high school in Richmond, Virginia.

Idolizing entertainers Grace Jones and Boy George, Aviance dreamed of one day being accepted by his peers and making a name for himself in the world of music. In the late 1990's, the powerhouse diva would make those dreams come true, but not without his fine share of hardships.

While residing in Washington, D.C. as a young adult, a crack addiction almost stopped Aviance in his tracks. Still going by the name "Eric Snead" at the time, the young impressionable lad would take solace and recovery in the House of Aviance and then adopt the name in its honor.

Aviance left Washington, D.C. for the lights and fame of New York City and created the hits, "Din Da Daa", "Rhythm Is My Bitch", "Alive", "Give It Up", and "Strut." The songs were no strangers to the Billboard dance chart – all of the singles reaching the #1 spot. Performing drag as a gay African American individual became his bread-and-butter job.

Then, in 1999, Aviance would star as a singer opposite voluminous award-winning actor Robert DeNiro in the Screen Actors Guild Award-nominated film Flawless. He would follow-up this performance starring as "Miss Smokie" in the 2000 film Punks (co-stars were Seth Gilliam and Andre Johnson). With guest appearances on The Tyra Banks Show and America's Next Top Model, Aviance appeared to be on the top of the world, but that would all change.

While exiting the New York City nightclub Phoenix on June 10, 2006, Aviance was attacked by a group of men flinging anti-gay slurs in his direction. Out of the assailants, four of them admitted foul-play and were prosecuted for up to 15 years in prison. The hate crime survivor would walk away with his life still intact, but the event would change him forever. He would go back to using drugs in the form of crystal methamphetamine.

Aviance said at the time, "It got crazy. I was drinking, drugging, shopping to sex to everything. I was trying to fill this void in my life. Crystal meth was the one thing that took me over the edge. I was doing it to keep myself going. I had to get outside my head."

Aviance made the conscious decision to change his life for the better, get clean and...design shoes. Of the fashion project Aviance told the New York Blade, "I've always wanted to be a designer and to go in that fashion world. I have a big fetish for high heels. The inspiration is my mother and other fierce women in my life. I'm dedicating my first collection to them."

[12] *Photo by Dan Couto*

TRACY CHAPMAN

Four-time Grammy Award-winning multi-platinum recording artist Tracy Chapman picked up the guitar at the impressionable age of eight years old and subsequently began to change the world one chord at a time. Her modest upbringing in a single-mother household with very little money or resources propelled Chapman to dig deep and channel her harrowing experiences through songwriting and music. She was one of the first African American singer-songwriters to openly discuss race, politics, segregation, and slavery in modern-day music.

Chapman was born in Cleveland, Ohio on March 30, 1964. She was accepted into the prestigious and private, co-educational Wooster School in Danbury, Connecticut before attending Tufts University near Boston, Massachusetts. She graduated in 1987 with a B.A. degree in anthropology and African studies. Years later, in 2004, Tufts University would award Chapman with an honorary Doctor of Fine Arts degree to celebrate her committed contributions to society throughout her music career.

Harvard Square in Cambridge, Massachusetts became Chapman's stomping ground in the early days leading up to her first recording contract. The expansive triangular area in the heart of the populous city showcased the best up-and-coming artists as they stood with anticipation only a stone's throw away from famed Harvard University. Chapman signed a record deal with Elektra Records in 1987.

Chapman was invited to sing her first hit off her debut album, Tracy Chapman, at the televised Nelson Mandela 70th Birthday Tribute concert in June 1988. "Fast Car" would go on to earn her a Grammy Award for "Best Female Pop Vocal Performance" in 1989 and a large fan following in the United States would become the result. Three more Grammy Awards would follow, including: Grammy Award for "Best New Artist" in 1989, Grammy Award for "Best Contemporary Folk Album" for Tracy Chapman also in 1989 and Grammy Award for "Best Rock Song" for "Give Me One Reason" in 1997. A total of eight studio albums were released throughout Chapman's career.

In 2008, Chapman composed original music for an acclaimed play by Athol Fugard with the subject of apartheid in South Africa at its core. The American Conservatory Theater's production of Blood Knot was the successful result of this collaborative effort.

While she has never chosen to publicly discuss her sexuality with the press, instead focusing on her music in interviews, Chapman has been linked to The Color Purple author Alice Walker, among other women. When the subject of their affair in the 1990's came up in an interview with Walker for The Guardian, Walker recalled that their affair was never really a secret. "It was quiet to you maybe but that's because you didn't live in our area." Walker has kept journals recounting her romantic relationship with Chapman and hopes to release them in the future.

[13] *Photo provided by Atlantic Records*

ALICE WALKER

2006 California Hall of Fame inductee Alice Walker is best known for her authorship of The Color Purple. The 1982 classic novel based on her own life story won the civil rights activist and essayist both the Pulitzer Prize for Fiction and the National book Award in 1983. Walker was the first black woman to ever win either award.

The Color Purple would eventually become both a film (in 1985 directed by Steven Spielberg) and Broadway stage production (in 2005 produced by Oprah Winfrey, Scott Sanders and Quincy Jones). Overall, The Color Purple would receive 11 Tony Award nominations with one win, five Outer Critics Circle Award nominations, three Drama League Award nominations, three Theatre World Award wins, one Grammy Award nomination, 12 NAACP Theatre Award nominations with three wins, 11 Academy Award nominations, five Golden Globe nominations with one win, and numerous other accolades. Steven Spielberg would win his first Directors Guild of America Award for Best Motion Picture Director for The Color Purple.

Walker was born to field worker parents in Eatonton, Georgia on February 9, 1944 during a time when the Jim

Crow Laws of 1876 through 1965 restricted the lives of African American people in the South. The separate-but-equal racial segregation laws prevented the black population in the United States from interacting with the white population in public schools, restaurants, places of worship, restrooms, transportation, and so on. Walker's mother enrolled her into first grade at the age of four in order to prevent her young daughter from working in the fields. She would go on to excel throughout her school years and become valedictorian of her high school class.

With the civil rights movement in full-force and the fire of activism running through her veins, Walker was inspired to attend the historic 1963 March on Washington where Martin Luther King, Jr. would deliver his monumental "I Have a Dream" speech to an estimated 300,000 people.

In 2003 on the eve of the Iraq war, Walker was arrested with 24 other protesters in Washington, D.C. Walker recalled, "I was with other women who believe that the women and children of Iraq are just as dear as the women and children in our families, and that, in fact, we are one family. And so it would have felt to me that we were going over to actually bomb ourselves." Walker's entire report of the matter can be found in her essay "We Are the Ones We Have Been Waiting For."

Furthering her commitment to the civil rights movement and her heritage, Walker donated 122 boxes of manuscripts and archive material to Atlanta, Georgia's Emory University's Manuscript, Archives, and Rare Book Library (MARBL) in 2007.

When President Barack Obama was sworn into office, Walker wrote a letter to him titled, "An Open Letter to Barack Obama." With references to the President as "Brother Obama," Walker wrote, "seeing you take your rightful place, based solely on your wisdom, stamina, and character, is a balm for the weary warriors of hope, previously only sung about."

Walker has one daughter from a previous marriage to Jewish civil rights lawyer Melvyn Roseman Leventhal. Her romance in the 1990's with singer-songwriter Tracy Chapman has been documented throughout unreleased journals maintained by Walker. Of the muted relationship, Walker has told the press, "It was quiet to you maybe but that's because you didn't live in our area."

[14] *Photo originally published on Wikipedia.org*

RUPAUL

RuPaul Andre Charles put it best when he said in his own words, "You can call me he. You can call me she. You can call me Regis and Kathie Lee; I don't care! Just as long as you call me." Popularly referenced in the entertainment industry as simply RuPaul, the world's first drag queen supermodel for MAC Cosmetics (or any other company) hit the ground running with the international dance classic, "Supermodel (You Better Work)" via Tommy Boy Records. His follow-up singles "A Shade Shady (Now Prance)" and "Back to My Roots" both went #1 on the Billboard Hot Dance Music/Club Play charts in 1993. That same year, a remake of "Don't Go Breaking My Heart" with Elton John would land RuPaul the highest single of his career on the UK Singles Chart (it went to spot #7). In total, the outspoken singer-songwriter would release four studio albums and one holiday album between the years 1993 and 2009.

Born in San Diego, California on November 17, 1960, RuPaul was raised as a "little adult" and had three female siblings. With their mother and father fighting a lot of the time, the children would run and hide in their bedrooms and look after one another. RuPaul has said of this formative time, "The divorce was as ugly and nasty as it could have gotten. I thought it was all my fault. I wouldn't understand how traumatized I was by it until I was well into my twenties. My mother basically shut down for a couple of years – isolating in her room with Valium and Lithium. We went on welfare and we kids became little adults, taking care of mom and keeping secrets from social workers, daddy and anyone else who could threaten our family."

When he came out in his twenties, RuPaul encountered hardship. He wrote, "I had moved to midtown that summer and lived with my first boyfriend, Todd. We had a rocky relationship which proved to me that I had learned more from my parents than I thought or cared to. It's no wonder why it had taken me so long to hook up."

Perhaps best known for his role in producing the reality game show RuPaul's Drag Race, RuPaul became a household name utilizing his talents for placement, pop, and pizzazz. MTV-owned lesbian, gay, bisexual and transgender (LGBT) channel Logo premiered the one-of-a-kind fashion adventure show on February 2, 2009. The first season of RuPaul's Drag Race was considered the most successful launch for the three-year-old Logo network. Traffic to the show's website broke records and RuPaul was front page news. A feat never accomplished by a drag queen before him (African American or otherwise).

RuPaul released his 2009 album Champion directly to iTunes and Amazon and it shot to the #1 spot on the iTunes Dance Album chart with singles, "Cover Girl" and "Jealous of My Boogie." RuPaul premiered his second reality television show for Logo called RuPaul's Drag U on July 19, 2010.

[15] *Photo by David Shankbone*

LINDA VILLAROSA

Editor, author, journalist and public speaker Linda Villarosa has received distinguished recognition for her work in the African American and lesbian, gay, bisexual and transgender communities. Among the honors bestowed upon Villarosa were awards from The American Medical Writers' Association, The Arthur Ashe Institute, Lincoln University, the New York Association of Black Journalists, the National Women's Political Caucus, the National Lesbian and Gay Journalists' Association and the Callen-Lorde Community Health Center.

Villarosa has contributed her time and talent to national magazines throughout her career including the very popular publications Glamour, Health, Latina, the New York Times Book Review, Essence Magazine, Science Times, O Magazine, Vibe and Woman's Day. Her column on the lesbian website AfterEllen is called "Outside the Lines" and she is a regular contributor to the daily online magazine for black audiences called The Root.

Born on January 9, 1959, Villarosa always suspected that she was different from the other girls. Although she served on the cheerleading squad during high school, ran on the track team, wore dresses, and dated boys, she felt apart from the other girls in her class.

The University of Colorado graduate released her very first novel to the world in 2008. It was titled, "Passing for Black" and it earned the ambitious journalist a Lambda Literary Award nomination. In an interview with SheWrites, the author shared, "I wanted to write a book about passing, but didn't want it to be historical fiction. I think of it as a coming-out story with the larger theme of passing. I was inspired by the work of early 20th-century authors Nella Larsen and Charles Chesnutt. Passing is also part of my own history: My mixed-race grandmother "passed for white," in a town outside of Chicago in the 1950s and '60s, causing a long and painful rift in our family."

In addition to "Passing for Black," Villarosa has written or co-written numerous additional literary works. She also lends her support to companies and organizations seeking editorial consultation and instruction, including: American Express Publishing, Dr. Phil, the Kaiser Family Foundation, and the Meredith Corporation. Villarosa also trained journalists from around the world to better cover the international HIV/AIDS epidemic and cover the International AIDS conferences in Barcelona, Bangkok and Toronto.

Villarosa came out of the closet in the early 1990's in Essence Magazine. She and her partner live in Brooklyn, New York with their two children. She also serves as the program director in the journalism department at the City College of New York (CCNY).

[16] *Photo courtesy Linda Villarosa.*

DOUG SPEARMAN

Noah's Arc actor Doug Spearman has been a gay rights advocate since he was a child growing up in Washington, D.C. In fact, he was born into the prime timeframe of the civil rights movement in 1962 – one year before Martin Luther King, Jr. would share his "I Have a Dream" speech in the very same city.

On August 10, 2009, HRC Backstory would release an essay by Spearman. Including his thoughts on the racial divide within the lesbian, gay, bisexual and transgender (LGBT) communities. Portions of his essay, titled Equality

Forward: A National Conversation about Race, Sexuality and Gender, follow below:

"People tend to believe that racism, on all sides of the color lines, is something that stops at the gates of the LGBT community. As though at the entrance to the various Boys Towns around the country you were required to check your ideas about Blacks, Asians, Jews, Arabs, etc... the way cowboys were required to turn over their guns when they walked into a salon in the Old West. It just doesn't happen that way. In fact, I think it's worse now than it was when I came out in 1980. Back then the bars felt a lot more friendly, prejudice was a dirty word, and the kids of the 1960's and early 70's – those that had created the gay movement – were still on the dance floors of America elbow to elbow with the people who'd marched in Vietnam protests and Black Power parades, and had been active participants in the original Civil Rights Movement. Those were the grownups who were standing at the bar when I got there. They welcomed me. But they're gone. That spirit seems to have evaporated. Not everywhere and not for everyone, but enough so that if you're over the age of thirty-five you would notice."

He continued, "It's a different world for white Americans than it is for black, brown, and yellow Americans. Especially if you have education, income, and available resources. And we're finally beginning to openly talk about the differences. Until we do, until we acknowledge the realities of all the -isms that exist within the LGBT community, we will never be able to face the discrimination and hatred that is aimed at us. Until we realize that the civil rights inequalities exist within the very worlds we've designed for ourselves then we've really just recreated the places a lot of us tried to escape from. Until rice queen and snow queen disappear from our own vocabularies, and until I don't have to overhear two white guys describe me as Mandingo (as I did in a club in LA one night) then we're not much better than the people out there who stand on corners with signs that say God Hates Fags."

Spearman is best-known for his role in Noah's Arc – A show on MTV's Logo network chronicling the lives of gay black men dealing with love, relationships, gay marriage, gay-bashing, and acceptance. He has also had roles on Star Trek Voyager, The Drew Carey Show, The Hughleys, Charmed, Gideon's Crossing, MAD TV, Girlfriends and Profiler. He currently serves on the Board of Equality California.

[17] *Photography by David Ross.*

SHERYL SWOOPES

Texan Sheryl Swoopes was the very first African American woman chosen for the Womens National Basketball Association (WNBA) during the league's inaugural season draft in 1997. The athlete's impressive 11-year span with the Houston Comets scored the star forward numerous slam dunk titles including three WNBA MVP awards (2000, 2002, 2005), three WNBA -Defensive Player of the Year awards (2000, 2002, 2003), and four WNBA champion titles (1997-2000). Swoopes is the second player in WNBA history to win both the regular season MVP award and the All-Star Game MVP award in the same season (the first player to win the award was Los Angeles Sparks' Lisa Leslie-Lockwood).

Swoopes led the U.S. to win the bronze medal in 2006 when the WNT team competed in Brazil during the World Championship.

The Seattle Storm signed Swoopes to their all-star WNBA team (including players Sue Bird and Lauren Jackson) on March 3, 2008. She played with the team for one season.

An international career brought success to Swoopes' doorstep as well. She joined the Russian basketball team VBM-SGAU Samara for their 2004-2005 seasons, the Italian basketball team Taranto Cras Basket from 2005-2006 and Greece's Esperides Kallitheas team in 2010.

Born in Brownsfield, Texas in 1971, Swoopes was raised by her mother, Louise Swoopes, and three older brothers. She married her high school sweetheart in 1995 and had a son they named Jordan Eric Jackson in 1997. Almost eight years later in October 2005, Swoopes made the announcement that she was gay. She would quickly become the most decorated WNBA player to ever make this announcement.

Swoopes is currently living in the state of Washington with her son and partner – former basketball player and Houston Comets assistant coach – Alisa Scott.

[18] *Photo provided by the Seattle Storm*

JOHN AMAECHI

John Amaechi became the first undrafted free agent to start the opening game of an NBA season and the first player in the NBA to out himself as a gay man. The retired Cleveland Cavaliers NBA decorated player admitted that he was gay via his controversially revealing memoir Man in the Middle (ESPN Books, 2007). No other NBA player regardless of color had accomplished this feat prior to Amaechi.

Originally met with disbelief and unfortunate wrath by his former teammates and acquaintances, Amaechi's very public coming out was later recognized within both the

LGBT and black communities as a very important step towards equality in America and around the world.

Amaechi was born to a Nigerian father and English mother on November 26, 1970 in Boston, Massachusetts. The family moved to Stockport, England when Amaechi was three years old. He remained in England until U.S. basketball beckoned and he returned to the states to settle in Toledo, Ohio. He would go on to attend St. John's Jesuit High School before signing up at Vanderbilt University in Nashville, Tennessee to try his luck there. Amaechi ultimately made the decision one year later to transfer to Penn State and became a two-time First Team Academic All-American selection. Pennsylvania agreed with the 6-foot-10-in. 270 lb. basketball player.

The Big Ten Conference website in 2009 asked Amaechi how he got his start in American basketball. He replied:

"I was walking down Market Street in Manchester [England] one day and some men asked me if I would be interested in playing basketball. At the time, I was a 6-foot-9, fat black kid and was one of only two brown kids (the other was from India) in my school. I was a real geek and really felt alone at the time, but through basketball I suddenly became a commodity. I remember writing in my high school yearbook that I wanted to play for the NBA championship and earn a lot of money. It was pretty vacuous thinking for a teenager."

Amaechi had bigger goals in life than just playing basketball. He wanted to become a psychologist, motivational speaker, political activist, and broadcaster. Penn State backed him up on his ambitious journey into changing the world.

"At Penn State, they knew how to map out a plan for me to become a psychologist because even though the NBA would be a wonderful world, it would not define my career," Amaechi said in the same 2009 interview with The Big Ten Conference website. "That plan involved a lighter load during the busiest time of my sport so I wouldn't have to get up for a bunch of 8 a.m. classes and be too tired to perform both on the court and in the classroom."

With his NBA career now behind him, Amaechi owns and runs Animus Consulting, which provides motivational speakers, and is back in school to get his Ph. D. in psychology.

19 Photo ©2006 Robert Severi

WANDA SYKES

Multiple Emmy Award winning actress, writer and comedienne Wanda Sykes was the first-ever African American and openly gay featured entertainer invited to attend the annual White House Correspondents' Association dinner in 2009. Forever quick with a quip or two, Sykes came barreling out of the proverbial closet in 2008 while speaking at an LGBT conference in support of marriage equality in Las Vegas, NV. She surprised the attendees at the rally by boisterously sharing, "I'm proud to be a woman. I'm proud to be a black woman and I'm proud to be gay."

Sykes was born on March 7, 1964 in Portsmouth, VA and was later raised in Washington, D.C. by her military dad and banker mom. Sykes toyed with the idea of entering the Armed Services herself when she enrolled in the National Security Agency and served for five years before moving on to trying her hand at stand-up comedy in New York City. Her big break came when she was asked to open for Chris Rock at New York's famed

Caroline's Comedy Club (she would later be signed to Chris Rock's writing team when he created his very own television show called The Chris Rock Show).

Numerous television show and film guest starring appearances would follow including: Pootie Tang, Curb Your Enthusiasm, Wanda at Large, Tongue Untied, Premium Blend, Wanda Does It, Evan Almighty, The Wanda Sykes Show, and most recently, The New Adventures of Old Christine. In addition to film, television and stage appearances, Sykes published a book titled, "Yeah, I Said It" in September 2004 through the Atria publishing group. Her writing credits are furthered by her literary participation in the 74th Annual Academy Awards presentation.

Throwing herself into the tenacious fight for equality, Sykes joined musician Cyndi Lauper's True Colors Tour as a performer in 2008 and, in that same year, offered her face and likeness to a television ad for the group GLSEN (Gay, Lesbian, and Straight Education Network).

Sykes is married to longtime partner Alex and the two women share the same legal last name. Their twins, named Olivia Lou and Lucas Claude, were born on April 27, 2009.

[20] *Photo of Wanda Sykes by Greg Hernandez.*

ABOUT THE AUTHORS

Leyla Farah

Leyla Farah is a Founding Partner at Cause+Effect, a media and marketing firm focused exclusively on the lesbian, gay, bisexual and transgender (LGBT) community.

Prior to founding Cause+Effect, she served as the Vice President of Programming and Production for PlanetOut Inc., where she oversaw the daily publication of news and feature stories for LGBT audiences around the world. With a background in corporate strategy, branding, communications, and software systems development, Leyla is uniquely positioned to comment on the convergence of digital communications, user-generated content, niche-market media, race and sexuality in modern society.

Leyla holds a JD from Boalt Hall School of Law at UC Berkeley and a BA from the Robert D. Clark Honors College at the University of Oregon. She has served on the national Board of Governors for the Human Rights Campaign, and as a volunteer with numerous LGBT arts and policy organizations around the country.

Sarah Toce

Sarah Toce is the Editor-in-Chief of The Seattle Lesbian and has been interviewed and recognized by Curve, GLAAD, SheWired, GLSEN, the San Diego Gay & Lesbian News, HIVster, Gay City Health Project, KIRO FM and more.

Some of Sarah's notable celebrity interviews include: Joy Behar, Cyndi Lauper, Chely Wright, Amy Ray, Sarah McLachlan, Bruce Vilanch, Sara Ramirez, Hal Sparks, Colbie Caillat, Jessica Clark, Nicole Pacent, Butterfly Boucher, Courtenay Semel, Brandi Carlile, Suzanne Westenhoefer, the cast of "Hannah Free", MTV's "The Buried Life," the No H8 Campaign's Jeff Parshley and Adam Bouska, and others. In addition to her interview with Adam and Jeff, Sarah posed for the campaign.

Sarah is a graduate from the New York Conservatory of Dramatic Arts in New York City. Her specialty is conducting celebrity interviews and covering high-profile events with a strong emphasis on political, social and LGBTQ-oriented topics.

INDEX

Every effort was made to identify and contact the owners of copyrighted materials, specifically including photos, prior to publication. Materials in the public domain were used when permission could not be obtained for copyrighted works.

If you feel this book contains material for which you hold legal copyright, or if you feel this book contains information which you believe to be factually inaccurate, please contact the authors via their representatives at Cause+Effect Public Relations.

Cause+Effect
www.cause-pr.com
info@cause-pr.com
866.843.6697 [fax]

For more information about this book or its authors, please visit www.blackgiftedandgay.com.

1 *Photography by David Christopher Lee. Photo originally published in Destination Luxury. -- http://www.destinationluxury.com/united-states/los-angeles/exclusive-interview-with-lee-daniels/ . Photo used with permission.*

2 *Photo of Angela Davis by Nick Wiebe. http://en.wikipedia.org/wiki/File:Angela-Davis-Mar-28-2006.jpg Used with permission under the Creative Commons Attribution-Share Alike 3.0 Unported license.*

3 *Photo courtesy Felicia "Snoop" Pearson. Used with permission.*

4 *Photo by David Shankbone (http://commons.wikimedia.org/wiki/File:Andre_Leon_Talley_at_the_2009_Tribeca_Film_Festival.jpg) [CC-BY-3.0 (www.creativecommons.org/licenses/by/3.0)], via Wikimedia Commons.*

5 *Photo courtesy Maurice Jamal. Used with permission.*

6 *Photo courtesy Emil Wilbekin. Used with permission.*

7 *Photo by Richard Berg [CC-BY-3.0 (www.creativecommons.org/licenses/by/3.0)], via Wikimedia Commons.*

8 *Photography by Yoon S. Byun/Globe Staff originally published at Boston.com. -- http://www.boston.com/news/education/higher/articles/2009/08/01/gates_case_stirs_up_cambridge_politics/ Photo used with permission.*

9 *Photo courtesy ESPN. Photo used with permission.*

10 *Photography by Mark Seliger. -- http://www.markseliger.com/ Photo used with permission.*

11 *Photo originally published on BET.com -- http://www.bet.com/News/news_noahsarcnominatedforimageaward.htm Copyright holder unreachable at date of publication.*

12 *Photo by Dan Couto Photography -- http://www.dancouto.com/. Photo used with permission.*

13 *Photo provided for public use by Atlantic Records -- http://www.atlanticrecords.com/tracychapman/photos*

[14] *Photo originally published on Wikipedia.org under a Creative Commons Attribution license. -- http://en.wikipedia.org/wiki/File:Alice_Walker,_1989.jpg*

[15] *Photo by David Shankbone via Wikimedia Commons - http://commons.wikimedia.org/wiki/File:RuPaul_by_David_Shankbone.jpg*

[16] *Photo originally published at LindaVillarosa.com. -- http://www.lindavillarosa.com/ Photo used with permission.*

[17] *Photography by David Ross. Photo used with permission.*

[18] *Photo provided for public use by the Seattle Storm. http://www.wnba.com/media/storm/swoopes_wp08_1024.jpg*

[19] *Photo ©2006 Robert Severi. http://www.robertseveri.com. Photo used with permission.*

[20] *Photo of Wanda Sykes at 2010 GLAAD Media Awards by Greg Hernandez. http://en.wikipedia.org/wiki/File:Wanda_Sykes_2010_GLAAD_Media_Awards.jpg Used with permission under the Creative Commons Attribution 2.0 Generic license.*

Made in the USA
San Bernardino, CA
22 January 2014